# Shakespeare's
# Flowers

# Shakespeare's Flowers

BY *Jessica Kerr*
ILLUSTRATED BY *Anne Ophelia Dowden*

*Johnson Books*
BOULDER

Published in the United States by Johnson Books, a division of Johnson Publishing Company, 1880 South 57th Court, Boulder, Colorado 80301.

9   8   7   6   5   4   3   2   1

Library of Congress Cataloging-in-Publication Data
Kerr, Jessica.
    Shakespeare's flowers / by Jessica Kerr: illustrated by Anne Ophelia Dowden.
        p.      cm.
    Originally published: New York: T. Crowell, 1969.
    Includes bibliographical references and indexes.
    ISBN 1-55566-202-1 (pbk.: alk. paper)
    1. Shakespeare, William, 1564–1616—Knowledge—Botany. 2. Flowers in literature. I. Dowden, Anne Ophelia Todd, 1907–   . II. Title.
PR3041.K4   1997
822.3'3—DC21                                                    97-22010
                                                                    CIP

Printed in the United States by
Johnson Printing
1880 South 57th Court
Boulder, Colorado 80301

 Printed on recycled paper

This book is dedicated by both author and artist
to Gertrude B. Foster,
with appreciation and gratitude.

## ACKNOWLEDGMENTS

The author and the artist wish to thank the following for assistance in the preparation of *Shakespeare's Flowers:*

The Ashmolean Museum, Oxford University; Mrs. Thelma Barton, Kent Memorial Library, Kent, Connecticut; the Bodleian Library, Oxford University; the Brooklyn Botanical Gardens, Mr. George Kalmbacher, Mr. Frederick McGourty, Mr. Peter Malins, Miss Jo-Ann Leevers; the College of Arms, London; the Folger Shakespeare Library, Washington, D.C.; Mr. H. Lincoln Foster, Falls Village, Connecticut; Dr. Levi Fox, O.B.E., Director of the Shakespeare Birthplace Trust, Stratford-upon-Avon; Miss Esther Ann Heubner, the Cloisters Museum, New York City; the Kent School Library, Kent, Connecticut; the Director of Kew Gardens, England; the New Milford Public Library, New Milford, Connecticut; Mrs. Dorothy Stanton of Cornwall, Connecticut, for the generous loan of many books; Mrs. Ella Statham, for cowslips sent from Surrey, England; Mrs. Mildred Van Vlack, Canaan, Connecticut; the Widener Library, Harvard University; the Lord Mayor of York, England.

*Flora of the British Isles* by A. R. Clapham, T. G. Tutin, and E. F. Warburg and *The Dictionary of Gardening of the Royal Horticultural Society* have been our authorities for botanical details. The quotations from Shakespeare follow the text of *The Yale Shakespeare.*

JESSICA KERR
ANNE OPHELIA DOWDEN

# CONTENTS

# Shakespeare's Flowers

# "THE FLOWERS ARE SWEET"

Why has this book been written? Perhaps because William Shakespeare was so very much a man of the time in which he lived and because he has described for us so vividly the England of Queen Elizabeth I four hundred years ago. From his plays we can learn about the people and their customs in town or country, the clothes they wore, the food they ate, and the fun and sport they enjoyed. We can read of the courage of soldiers and sailors and explorers, and the men who carried their trade across the sea into strange and distant lands. We can observe the intrigues of the court. Above all, we get a wonderful picture of the English countryside and of the gardens and flowers which are the subject of this book.

William Shakespeare grew up as a country boy and never lost his love for flowers. The house where he was born must have had a garden, even if a small one, with an all-important herb garden and, perhaps, an orchard at the back. The market town of Stratford was very small when Shakespeare lived there, and the wide flowery meadows, the woods, and the broad river Avon were only a few minutes' walk from his house in Henley Street. A little farther away were some of the great houses of Warwickshire, with splendid formal gardens, masterpieces of planting and design. These, as well as the famous gardens sloping down to the bank of the river Thames in London, the poet must have seen many a time.

Shakespeare liked to use flowers as images to illustrate his ideas about people—from kings and queens, and even whole nations, to the humble "burgesses" of his own town—what they looked like, their characters, and their actions. He used many other country images, too, such as birds, sports, music, and the seasons of the year. But above all he used flowers and, for the most part, the same wild flowers which still grow in the fields or by the river near his home.

Shakespeare left Stratford some time between 1585 and 1589, perhaps in the great year of the Spanish Armada; we do not know for certain. But he came back, famous and popular, to spend his last years in the fine house with its charming garden which he bought when success came to him.

England in his day was full of fears and superstitions. People believed in fairies and witches, poison brews, love potions, spells and signs and mysterious portents in the heavens, omens of disaster and dark forebodings. All this was familiar to Shakespeare, and so we find Puck and "the little people" (as the fairies were often called) in *A Midsummer Night's Dream*; the Three Witches in *Macbeth*; the Ghost in *Hamlet*; and the very convincing mischief of Caliban and Ariel in *The Tempest*. Shakespeare knew that the bunch of dried herbs or "simples" hanging from a nail in his mother's kitchen could be used not only to sweeten the pot or as salve for a wound but also, when prepared by witches, to destroy or bewitch.

A few of Shakespeare's plays do not mention flowers at all; others do so only occasionally. But there are plenty of flowers in his later plays, especially in *The Winter's Tale*, which was written when the poet was living in his own house in Stratford and was much preoccupied with the growing and planting of trees and flowers. *A Midsummer Night's Dream* is another play that is full of flowers, possibly because in Shakespeare's mind fairies and flowers were inseparable!

The flowers that Shakespeare loved best were the flowers of his childhood and his home. These were the ones he chose "to hold, as 'twere, the mirror up to nature."

GILLYVORS

CARNATION

4

CARNATION
GILLYVOR

*Sir, the year growing ancient,*
*Not yet on summer's death, nor on the*
    *birth*
*Of trembling winter, the fairest flowers o'*
    *the season*
*Are our carnations, and streak'd gillyvors.*
        —THE WINTER'S TALE

*PINKS*

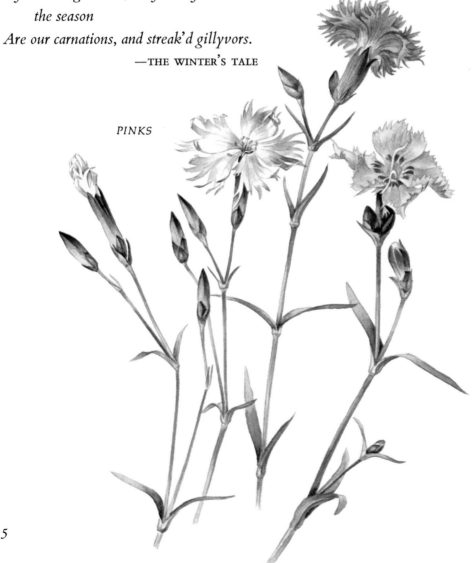

5

The carnation has been a favourite in English gardens for many hundreds of years. Indeed, it is said to have been brought to Britain by the Romans, who invaded the country in 55 B.C. under Julius Caesar and occupied it for more than four hundred years. The carnation was used in Italy for wreaths and garlands—known in Latin as *corona*; and the flower, first known in England as "coronation," gradually came to be called "carnation." A story is told of a Roman soldier who brought the seeds of the carnation to England in the mud on his boots. But it is more likely that Roman soldiers carried the seeds of the flower with them and planted them, much as the Pilgrim Fathers did the seeds they brought from England to their new home in America.

Carnations and "gillyvors" belong to the same species, of which the carnation, which we know so well in florists' shops, is the largest and most splendid. There were many strange and varied spellings of "gillyvor." The poet Chaucer, writing two hundred years before Shakespeare, called it "gylofre," and in France it was called "girofle." But all versions of its name probably come from the Latin *Caryophyllus*, which means "cloves." The gillyflower was sometimes called "clove-gillyflower" because of its rich pungent smell. Its flowers were used to make a delicious wine, and for that reason it was also known as "sops-in-wine." There is an even smaller member of this species which we call the pink. It was customary to describe perfect manners as being "the very pink of courtesy" (*Romeo and Juliet*).

At the time that Shakespeare wrote *The Winter's Tale* he had left London and the theater behind him for good and returned to the fine house and garden in Stratford, where he was to end his days. So in this play there is much about gardens, flowers, and trees and about their care and cultivation. Like any good gardener Shakespeare thought a great deal about the seasons of the year. As a poet he compared them to the lives of men and women, from the springtime of childhood to the winter ("trembling winter" as he calls it) of old age. In this quotation from the play Perdita is talking about midsummer—middle age—and the flowers—carnations and gillyvors—which bloom in gardens at that time. "Streak'd gillyvors" were flowers of mixed colors developed by gardeners. In appearance they were mottled or variegated with patterns such as we find today in Sweet William or some garden pinks.

*DAISY*

DAISY
LADY-SMOCK
CUCKOO-BUD

*When daisies pied and violets blue,*
*    And lady-smocks all silver-white,*
*And cuckoo-buds of yellow hue*
*    Do paint the meadows with delight.*
                    —LOVE'S LABOUR'S LOST

LADY-SMOCK

CUCKOO-BUD
(buttercup)

9

More than one hundred and fifty years before Shakespeare was born, another great English poet, Geoffrey Chaucer, wrote with affection about the daisy, which he sometimes called "days-eye" and which he loved above all the flowers of the meadow. This little flower, with its round cheerful face, is quite different from the common daisy of American fields, though it does grow in an occasional garden. In England, fields and lawns and grassy slopes are thickly covered with it almost all year long. A daisy is included in Ophelia's garland in *Hamlet*, and in *The Two Noble Kinsmen* (a late play that Shakespeare may have written with John Fletcher) daisies are described as "smel-lesse, yet most quaint," the word "quaint" in those days meaning "pretty." In his poem "The Rape of Lucrece" Shakespeare describes the "perfect white" of his heroine's hand as showing "like an April daisy on the grass." This poetic image of a daisy suggests that Shakespeare knew that the daisy is the "month-flower" of April.

Lady-smock is another flower of early spring and of the meadow. It was also known as "cuckoo-flower," perhaps because it was in bloom at the time of year when the first clear notes of the cuckoo were heard. It is said that the name lady-smock was given to this flower because, although light pink or lavender in color, it appears as a silver-white carpet when spread over a meadow. To the poet's eye, it resembled the white smocks of ladies, spread out on the grass to bleach in the sun. Shakespeare mentions this in the same song:

> *When turtles tread, and rooks, and daws,*
> *And maidens bleach their summer smocks.*

The turtle in this song is the turtledove, strutting in the farmyard with the other fowl.

Just what flower was meant by the "cuckoo-bud" is a little uncertain, but it is generally thought to be the buttercup. The brilliant gold color of this most luxuriant of English wild flowers would, indeed, "paint the meadows with delight," and it is easy to believe that Shakespeare saw such a meadow in early spring and painted it in words, just as an artist paints a picture with his brush.

*HEMLOCK*

12

*Crown'd with rank fumitor and*
*furrow-weeds,*
*With burdocks, hemlock, nettles,*
*cuckoo-flowers,*
*Darnel and all the idle weeds that grow*
*In our sustaining corn.*
　　　　　　　—KING LEAR

*There with fantastic garlands did she come,*
*Of crowflowers, nettles, daisies.*
　　　　　　　—HAMLET

What gardener does not know about weeds! Shakespeare must have pulled up many of them in his garden at New Place, as any garden lover does today, and he learned about them from the farms and fields so near his boyhood home.

Gentle, mad Ophelia and wild, demented King Lear cover their heads with weeds and flowers from the riverside or the fields. This may seem strange until we understand that the wearing of wreaths and chaplets of flowers was a custom of Elizabethan times. Garlands were a mark of joy or sorrow at weddings and funerals. King Lear covers his wild gray hair with "rank fumitor," a weed which grows in cornfields. Fumitor, or fumitory, is a pretty little plant and lives longer than any other flower that grows in the furrow made by the plough. The word "rank" in Shakespeare's time meant luxuriant, *not* evil-smelling. Furrow-weeds like fumitory thrive in ploughed fields.

Hemlock does have a strong unpleasant smell. So bad was its reputation that it was said to be an ingredient of a witch's brew of the kind that we read about in *Macbeth*. Though it has always been known as a strong poison, hemlock is also valuable as a plant of healing.

Most people know about nettles, and their sharp sting is no less painful today than it was when the King in *Richard II* cried, "Yield stinging nettles to mine enemies." Nettles are, of course, among the most annoying of all weeds, but even so we find in them unexpected virtues.

*DARNEL*

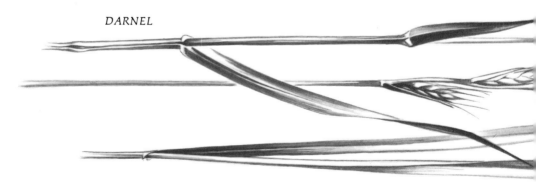

The famous diarist Samuel Pepys recorded in February 1661 that he "did eat some Nettle porridge . . . which was very good"!

The tares of which we read in the New Testament are said to be the same harmful weed that Shakespeare called darnel. It choked the corn and became mixed with the wheat and was the enemy of farmers, millers, and bakers. But darnel had another quality; it was said to cause blindness, or "dim-sight," which led to a saying that people who were "dim-sighted"—meaning "dim-witted"—had "eaten darnel." So Shakespeare included it in the weeds worn by King Lear with good reason.

There is one flower in Ophelia's "fantastic garland" that we have not met before. The crowflower is thought to be the pink flower known today as ragged robin, found where land is moist or marshy. Ophelia could have

*NETTLE*

16

CROWFLOWER
*(ragged robin)*

FUMITOR

17

picked crowflowers beside the river and twined them into her garland. They were used a great deal, we are told, for that purpose. The flowers in her sad garland could all have been observed by Shakespeare on an afternoon walk beside the river Avon.

Apart from these two garlands, Shakespeare thought of weeds as representing the bitter harvest of neglect, wasted years, and the devastation of war. He seems to feel that nettles grow where there should be flowers, just as there is often evil where good should be. Writing in *King Richard II* of England one hundred years before his time, he is thinking of the misgovernment and evil in his own country:

> *. . . I will go root away*
> *The noisome weeds, which without profit suck*
> *The soil's fertility from wholesome flowers.*

A few lines farther on in this great scene he says:

> *. . . our sea-walled garden, the whole land,*
> *Is full of weeds, her fairest flowers chok'd up.*

In any town or village where his plays were performed, Shakespeare was sure of a garden-loving audience who would well understand his feelings about "noisome weeds."

*Where the bee sucks, there suck I,*
*In a cowslip's bell I lie.*

—THE TEMPEST

*The cowslips tall her pensioners be;*
*In their gold coats spots you see;*
*Those be rubies, fairy favours,*
*In their freckles live their savours;*
*I must go seek some dewdrops here,*
*And hang a pearl in every cowslip's ear.*

—A MIDSUMMER NIGHT'S DREAM

In England the cowslip used to be the children's favorite flower. Each year in April they would go out with baskets to pick the blossoms in the fields and hedges and come home laden, to make "cowslip-balls" or "tossies." Tying the flowers together tightly at the top of the stalk in big bunches, they then cut away most of the stalk.

This happy pastime is no longer possible in many parts of England because the cowslip is becoming very scarce. For the same reason country people make less cowslip wine—a delicately flavored amber-colored drink, extracted from the nectar of the "freckles" inside the cup of the flower of which the Fairy speaks in *A Midsummer*

*Night's Dream*. In medieval times the leaves were used to make salads and the juice to soothe a cough.

This flower was a favorite of the fairies and was known as "the Fairies' cup." We get a good idea of the size of Oberon, king of the fairies, and of Titania, his queen, when we learn that Ariel could creep into the bell of one of the little yellow flowers on a stalk; and that the elves could "creep into acorn cups and hide them there."

Shakespeare's description of cowslips as "pensioners" of Titania is interesting because, as he well knew, Queen Elizabeth of England was always attended by fifty of the noblest, tallest, and handsomest of the young men at her court in London. Richly dressed and bedecked with jewels, they acted as her guard of honor, and were known

*COWSLIP*

as "Gentlemen Pensioners." Wherever the Queen traveled, her court went with her. Shakespeare might well have seen these splendid attendants when Queen Elizabeth made her famous visit to Kenilworth Castle when he was a small boy.

There is one sad reference to the cowslip in *Henry V*. The Duke of Burgundy speaks of the ruin and disorder into which the fair land of France has fallen through war and strife and of the "freckled cowslip" that the meadow used to bring "sweetly forth" and that is now lost among uncared-for grasses and weeds.

On the other hand, Shakespeare has a little joke— making fun of his own frequent use of flowers—in *A Midsummer Night's Dream*. Thisbe, in the wonderful comic play put on by Bottom and his rustic friends, recites:

> *These lily lips,*
> *This cherry nose,*
> *These yellow cowslip cheeks.*

Cowslips never grow wild in the United States, but they can be seen sometimes in gardens where they are known by the scientific name *Primula veris*. They are first cousins of the primroses and oxlips.

*. . . and there is pansies, that's for thoughts.*
—HAMLET

*Yet mark'd I where the bolt of Cupid fell:*
*It fell upon a little western flower,*
*Before milk-white, now purple with love's*
*wound,*
*And maidens call it Love-in-idleness.*
—A MIDSUMMER NIGHT'S DREAM

The pansy to which poor Ophelia referred was not the flower we know by that name today. It was, in fact, the "little western flower" of *A Midsummer Night's Dream* described by Oberon, king of the fairies, as being once white, "now purple with love's wound." There is usually a touch of yellow also in this flower. It is known in this country as "Johnny-jump-up" and as heartsease in most parts of England, especially in Warwickshire where Shakespeare lived. The name pansy comes from *pensée,* the French word for thought, and is only used this one time by Shakespeare.

It has taken many years to cultivate the big round-faced pansy of today from the little "*Viola tricolor*" of Elizabethan England. The first true pansy is said to have been produced in a garden near London only about one hundred and fifty years ago. Yet it is this flower which most people have in mind when they read of the pansy handed by Ophelia to her brother as a symbol of lovers' thoughts.

Heartsease has many other quaint names such as "Three faces under a hood," "Tickle my fancy," or "Pink of my John." It is very possible that some of the early settlers in colonial times brought this little flower with them and gave it the name by which it is known in this country.

Shakespeare's name for it, "Love-in-idleness," is still used in parts of England and means "love in vain"; but Shakespeare is the only writer to call it "Cupid's flower." This is the little flower that Oberon tells Puck to find "ere the Leviathan can swim a league" and he instructs his fairy messenger to:

> Fetch me that flower; the herb I showed thee once:
> The juice of it on sleeping eyelids laid
> Will make or man or woman madly dote
> Upon the next live creature that it sees.

People in Shakespeare's day believed in the power of spells, charms, and magic potions—some, helpful and healing; others, mischievous and harmful. This flower,

PANSY
*(heartsease)*

WORMWOOD

25

which caused poor Queen Titania to become "enamoured of an ass," was a powerful love potion. Toward the end of the play, Oberon repents of his rather cruel jest and lifts the spell, restoring his queen to her normal self by touching her eyes with the juice of another herb:

> *Be as thou wast wont to be;*
> *See as thou wast wont to see:*
> *Dian's bud o'er Cupid's flower*
> *Hath such force and blessed power.*
> *Now, my Titania, wake you my sweet queen.*

This herb is thought to have been wormwood, the botanical name of which is artemisia after Artemis, the Greek goddess of the chase. The Roman counterpart of Artemis was Diana, but the name "Dian's bud" was probably invented by Shakespeare himself. Its magic power must have been more potent than that of love-in-idleness. By witches it was held that it could cure the bite of a sea-dragon!

Thomas Tusser, a farmer-poet of the sixteenth century, had other uses for wormwood:

> *While wormwood hath seed get a bundle or twain*
> *To save against March, to make flea to refrain.*
> *Where Chamber is swept and wormwood is strown,*
> *No flea for his life dare abide to be known.*

*And sometimes lurk I in a gossip's bowl,*
*In very likeness of a roasted crab;*
*And, when she drinks, against her lips I bob.*
      —A MIDSUMMER NIGHT'S DREAM

*When roasted crabs hiss in the bowl . . .*
      —LOVE'S LABOUR'S LOST

Many people reading these lines must be puzzled by the idea of a crab in a bowl of ale! The truth of the matter is that "crab" in this case is the name given by country people in Shakespeare's time to the little crab apple with its delicate flavor and pretty pink and white blossoms. In those days a "roasted crab" in a bowl of ale was a very popular Christmas dish.

A brew called "Lambs-wool," consisting of ale, nutmeg, sugar, and toasted crab apples, is still served at one of the colleges at Cambridge University in England. The strange name "Lambs-wool" has no connection with either lambs or their wool but comes from the name of a very old Celtic drink "Lamasaghel." It was drunk on the feast day of Lammastide, which falls on August first when the apples are ripening.

This brew was also popular at christenings. The god-parents were sometimes called "gossips," and the christening mug was known as "the gossips' bowl." The wassail bowl of the Christmas carols probably tasted very much the same, and it almost certainly had roasted crab apples in it.

*CRAB APPLE*

29

It is also confusing in *The Tempest* when Caliban says, "I prithee, let me bring thee where crabs grow." This scene is laid on an island, and it would be natural to picture crabs scrambling about on the seashore. But now we understand what Caliban meant, and how Puck, in *A Midsummer Night's Dream*, disguised by magic power as a crab apple, could bob up and down in an old lady's bowl of ale and cause her to spill her drink!

*What say'st thou, my fair flower-de-luce?*
—HENRY V

*. . . lilies of all kinds,*
*The fleur-de-luce being one.*
—THE WINTER'S TALE

Stratford-upon-Avon, as its name implies, is a town through which flows the beautiful river Avon. Shakespeare in his boyhood, and later when he walked a mile or so to Shottery to court Ann Hathaway, must have lingered on the banks of the river and observed the many wild flowers growing there. Among these would have been the tall iris with its bright colors of purple, yellow, or white. During the years he spent in London as actor and playwright, he could have seen the cultivated varieties of this flower in formal gardens there, but by that time he would have called it "flower-de-luce."

The name came from France, where the flower was called "fleur de Louis" after the French king Louis VII. He chose the yellow iris for the emblem on his shield and banner when he went on his first Crusade to the Holy Land in the twelfth century. When Edward III of England claimed the crown of France some two hundred

FLOWER-DE-LUCE
*(Florentine iris)*

32

years later he added the "fleur-de-lys" (as it had come to be called) to the English coat of arms. There, strangely enough, it remained until nearly two hundred and fifty years after Calais had been returned to France. Perhaps it just wasn't noticed! The loss of Calais is referred to in *Henry VI, Part I*:

> *Cropp'd are the flower-de-luces in your arms;*
> *Of England's coat one half is cut away.*

FLOWER-DE-LUCE
(*wild iris*)

English travelers were apt to be careless with regard to spelling and pronunciation, and so various versions of the name "fleur-de-lys" came back to England—flower-de-luce and flower-delice among them. Poets and writers sometimes took liberties in those days, and so we find Chaucer and Shakespeare occasionally confusing the lily with the iris.

The fleur-de-lys as it is often seen today in tapestry or carved on tombs in great cathedrals is really a heraldic symbol and not a true flower any more.

It is not possible to consider the flowers in Shakespeare's plays without some reference to French and English history. There are two reasons for this. First, Shakespeare chose historical subjects for some of his finest plays. Secondly, the destinies of the two countries had been closely linked for centuries, not only by travelers and diplomats but also by bitter and destructive wars between them.

Henry V calls Katharine of France "my fair flower-de-luce" just as he might have called her "my fair lily" in the famous scene where he tries to court her in a mixture of English and French. It would seem that Henry's name for Katharine was his attempt at being very gracious in French!

*Of all flowers*
*Methinks a rose is best.*
—THE TWO NOBLE KINSMEN

*So sweet a kiss the golden sun gives not*
*To those fresh morning drops upon the rose.*
—LOVE'S LABOUR'S LOST

*Let one attend him with a silver basin*
*Full of rose-water and bestrew'd with*
*     flowers.*
—THE TAMING OF THE SHREW

*. . . with two Provincial roses on my*
*     razed shoes.*
—HAMLET

In *Romeo and Juliet*, Juliet bewails the fate by which the name of Montague stands between her and Romeo and their happiness. She cries, "What's in a name? That which we call a rose by any other name would smell as sweet." But so universal is the love for the rose—queen of flowers and national emblem of England—that it has never had any other name.

Shakespeare mentions it at least seventy times in his

plays and sonnets, and in almost every case his meaning is quite clear. Like other poets of his time, he compares roses to human lips and cheeks, and uses them to suggest a blush of shame or anger. Some of his loveliest poetry is concerned with morning dew on the petals of roses, a sight that he must have often observed in his own garden or in the more splendid gardens of his friends in London. He would have known that the dew from rose petals was highly prized for the making of rare and costly cosmetics for Elizabethan ladies. Rose water, distilled from rose petals by apothecaries, especially in France, was much favored for bathing the face and hands, as we read in *The Taming of the Shrew*. Shakespeare was also very much aware of the all too short life of a rose in bud or in its full glory. He found in this a symbol of the sad fate that may befall youth and beauty from "killing frosts" or the

*PROVINCIAL ROSE*
*(cabbage rose)*

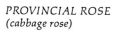

ravages of the cankerworm which particularly attacks roses. Queen Titania in *A Midsummer Night's Dream* dispatches her elves "to kill cankers in the musk-rose buds." In Shakespeare's time people lived very close to death, in a world full of war and plague. His many references to this subject prove how much the matter was in his thoughts.

When Hamlet speaks of wearing "two Provincial roses on my razed shoes," he is not referring to a fresh rose picked in the garden but to the rosettes, made of silk ribbon, which were much worn by gentlemen at the court of Queen Elizabeth. However, the kind of rose he mentions *is* a real rose, probably the Provençal cabbage rose. Perhaps he chose this flower to decorate his shoes, in mockery, because of its great size. There is another reference to this fashion in *Romeo and Juliet*, where Romeo says, "Why, then is my pump well flowered." He could have been speaking of a rosette on his shoe such as Hamlet wore.

Finally Shakespeare writes of the rose as part of English history, as indeed it is. In the play *Henry VI, Part I*, he depicts the scene that traditionally is supposed to have started the Wars of the Roses. In 1455 two rival houses, York and Lancaster, both claimed the crown of England.

Shakespeare has dramatized this moment in history in a long imaginary scene in the Temple garden in London. The rose might be said to play the leading role, as Richard Plantagenet for the House of York and the Earl of Somerset for the House of Lancaster both pluck a flower as a symbol of allegiance:

PLANTAGENET.  *Let him that is a true-born gentleman*
*And stands upon the honour of his birth,*
*If he suppose that I have pleaded truth,*
*From off this brier pluck a white rose with me.*

EARL OF  *Let him that is no coward and no flatterer,*
SOMERSET.  *But dare maintain the party of the truth,*
*Pluck a red rose from off this thorn with me.*

The prophetic words of the Earl of Warwick follow, summing up the scene he has just witnessed:

*And here I prophesy; this brawl to-day*
*Grown to this faction in the Temple garden,*
*Shall send between the red rose and the white*
*A thousand souls to death and deadly night.*

RED ROSE
*(Lancaster rose)*

After thirty-two years of bitter civil war the two fam-
ilies were united by the marriage of Henry VII to Elizabeth of York after the great battle of Bosworth Field. The
two roses, red and white, were joined in the symbolic
Tudor rose that still appears on the tombs of English
kings. There is also a red-and-white variety of the damask
rose—Shakespeare refers to it several times—that has
come to be known as the "York and Lancaster" rose.

*WHITE ROSE*
*(York rose)*

# PRIMROSE

*And in the wood where often you and I*
*Upon faint primrose-beds were wont to lie.*
—A MIDSUMMER NIGHT'S DREAM

*Whiles, like a puff'd and reckless libertine,*
*Himself the primrose path of dalliance*
*treads.*
—HAMLET

*The violets, cowslips, and the primroses*
*Bear to my closet.*
—CYMBELINE

There is always gladness in the sight of the first pale yellow primrose after a long winter. In *The Two Noble Kinsmen* it is called:

*Primrose, first-born child of Ver,*
*Merry spring-time's harbinger.*

("Ver" is an old name for spring, associated with the French word *vert* which means green. A "harbinger" is a messenger who runs ahead to proclaim that some person or event is on the way.) But Shakespeare does not often write so cheerfully about primroses. He calls them "faint" and "pale," and he sighs because they flower so early in

the year that they never live to see the summer sun—
"Bright Phoebus in his strength"—riding high in the sky.
It is strange that he should have chosen this frail sweet
flower to describe the downward path of evil-living, and
yet he does so twice—first in *Hamlet* and again in *Macbeth*
where the old porter at the castle gate says:

> *I had thought to have let in some . . . that go the primrose*
> *way to the everlasting bon-fire.*

Perhaps Shakespeare, like other poets of his time, thought
of sweet flowers underfoot as a tempting carpet for the
road to "everlasting fire"!

One thing is certain—Shakespeare thought often of
banks of primroses as pleasant places for men or fairies to
recline.

PRIMROSE

44

*That strain again! It had a dying fall;*
*O, it came o'er my ear like the sweet sound,*
*That breathes upon a bank of violets,*
*Stealing and giving odour.*

—TWELFTH NIGHT

*. . . I think the king is but a man, as I am;*
*the violet smells to him as it doth to me.*

—HENRY V

## VIOLET

The violet is one of the best loved of all flowers, whether it grows in a garden, in a wood, or on a bank. It is prized by poets for its perfume and sometimes pitied by them for the shortness of its life, for it is one of the very first flowers to appear with the coming of spring and seldom stays to enjoy the summer sunshine. For this reason it is often associated with death, like the primrose. It is described by Laertes in *Hamlet* as:

> *A violet in the youth of primy nature,*
> *Forward, not permanent, sweet, not lasting,*
> *The perfume and suppliance of a minute;*
> *No more.*

The word "forward" refers here to the violet's early flowering, not to its lack of modesty—it is the very emblem of modesty! "Suppliance" is a word no longer used today, but in Elizabethan times this phrase implied temporary pleasure or gratification.

When Perdita in *The Winter's Tale* speaks of "Violets dim, but sweeter than the lids of Juno's eyes," she is probably thinking of the custom among women in ancient Greece of painting their eyelids with a purple, sweet-scented ointment. The goddess Juno might well have used such an ointment.

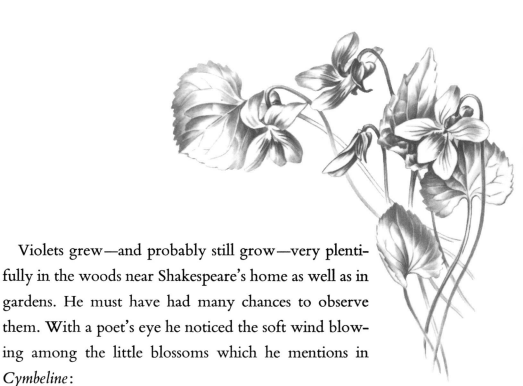

Violets grew—and probably still grow—very plentifully in the woods near Shakespeare's home as well as in gardens. He must have had many chances to observe them. With a poet's eye he noticed the soft wind blowing among the little blossoms which he mentions in *Cymbeline*:

> *. . . as gentle*
> *As zephyrs, blowing below the violet,*
> *Not wagging his sweet head.*

There is often a touch of sadness in Shakespeare's references to violets. One of the saddest is spoken by Ophelia:

> *. . . I would give you some violets, but they*
> *withered all when my father died.*

The tender, modest, sweet flower that Shakespeare loved so much could also die for sorrow.

FENNEL

COLUMBINE

48

*There's fennel for you and columbine.*

—HAMLET

In *Henry IV*, *Part II*, Falstaff describes Poins, one of his wild companions, as eating "conger and fennel"—an Elizabethan dish of eels and herbs—which he liked to share with Prince Hal. Fennel had other qualities—its peculiar aromatic flavor, for which it is used even today in fish dishes, and its reputation as the emblem of flattery. This was, no doubt, what Ophelia had in mind when she offered fennel to Laertes, and she may also have had in her mind the old country proverb, "Sow fennel, sow sorrow."

The old-fashioned columbine grew plentifully in cottage gardens and was known by the odd name of "Granny bonnet." It was thought to be a "thankless flower" and the emblem of forsaken lovers.

It must not be forgotten that the flowers in poor Ophelia's hands and in her wandering mind were mentioned by Shakespeare because of their association in folklore with certain human qualities usually connected with faithless lovers. Thus, fennel was the emblem of flattery, and columbine of ingratitude.

# RUE

*. . . there's rue for you, and here's some
for me; we may call it herb of grace
o' Sundays. O, you must wear your
rue with a difference.*

—HAMLET

When a person has said or done something which will sooner or later bring regret and repentance, he may be warned by a friend with the words, "You'll rue the day." Because repentance in Elizabethan times was associated with bitterness, the herb rue with its strong aromatic smell and the bitter, sour flavor of its leaves came to be associated with repentance, too. Countryfolk four hundred years ago believed that grace and forgiveness followed repentance, which is demonstrated by the other name given to the plant—"herb of grace o' Sundays."

In the sad lines spoken by the gardener in *King Richard II*, out of pity for the sorrow of the queen, we find rue again:

*Here did she fall a tear; here, in this place
I'll set a bank of rue, sour herb of grace:
Rue, even for ruth, here shortly shall be seen,
In the remembrance of a weeping queen.*

"Ruth" is an old word for pity, and so here we have grace and forgiveness and pity in four lovely lines of verse.

To "wear your rue with a difference," as Ophelia tells the King and Queen and her brother, Laertes, is a reference to the term "difference" used in heraldry to distinguish the coats of arms of different branches of the same family. So, as Ophelia points out, the repentance of the King and Queen must by reason of their exalted rank be different from hers.

In Shakespeare's day people lived in constant dread of the plague, which swept over England in fierce epidemics. Herbs, such as rosemary and rue, are still carried in the processions of the Lord Mayor of London as a traditional preventative against the plague, and a little nosegay of rue is placed beside a judge in court to this day. In the great city of York the wife of the Lord Mayor hands the judge a little silver container known as a "vinaigrette" containing strong aromatic herbs as he prepares to enter the courthouse. These customs go back to the grim days of the plague and the fear and horror of prison fevers.

RUE

52

## ROSEMARY

*There's rosemary, that's for remembrance;*
  *pray you, love, remember.*

—HAMLET

*For you there's rosemary and rue; these keep*
*Seeming and savour all the winter long;*
*Grace and remembrance be to you both.*

—THE WINTER'S TALE

53

The flowers that poor distraught Ophelia carries when she enters a room in the great castle of Elsinore were not chosen haphazardly by Shakespeare. Flowers and herbs of all kinds have always meant much to country people in England, providing remedies for sickness and wounds, as well as flavor for the pot. Medicinal herbs were called "simples," and herbs for the kitchen were known as "pot-herbs." People also believed that magic spells and love potions could be brewed from herbs, and witches were thought to be particularly skillful in this art. So they industriously cultivated herbs in their gardens for such purposes as well as for their stews and salads. In every Elizabethan house herbs hung from a nail to dry, and some of the larger houses kept herbs, both for flavor and as medicine, in a "still-room"—a name that comes from the process of "distilling" or extracting the juices, flavors, and essences of plants and herbs.

In sixteenth-century London the apothecaries, who kept the "drugstores" of Shakespeare's time, sold herbs and drugs as well as the much-favored spices from overseas and prescribed them for all kinds of illnesses. There was little medicine as the word is used today, and the apothecary, in his rich-smelling little shop with its herbs and simples, was an important man. When Shakespeare

54

lived in London, members of this trade may have been among his friends. In *The Merry Wives of Windsor* Falstaff makes an interesting reference to the London street where the apothecaries plied their business—a street known as Bucklesbury. Falstaff said that the overdressed and perfumed dandies of the court smelled "like Bucklesbury in simple-time." Indeed we are told that this street could be smelled from a long way off, so powerful was the odor of its herbs and spices. Shakespeare would have known it well. Two of his friends from Stratford-upon-Avon were apprenticed to a "pepperer" (the Elizabethan name for a grocer) living there and later set up business in the neighborhood on their own.

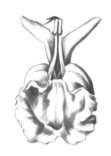

Rosemary is one of the best-loved herbs. We know it best for "remembrance" and as a fragrant addition to a stew. But it has also a long and honorable reputation as a remedy for many disorders of the body. Not so well known is the fact that the stem of the plant, when it had grown thick and tall against a garden wall, was used to make the beautiful lutes that provided so much of the music in Elizabethan England. And finally its evergreen leaves were a popular garnish for food and table at Christmastime.

But above all its many and varied uses, we associate

rosemary with faithfulness and remembrance. A little nosegay of the plant, bound together with gold silk or lace (known as "bride-lace"), was handed to the bridegroom on his wedding day by the friends of the bride at an Elizabethan marriage feast. A ballad of 1543 describes a wedding at which "there was a fair bride-cup of silver gilt carried before her [the bride] wherein was a goodly branch of rosemary . . . hung about with silken ribbons of all colours."

It is pleasant if one can find a sprig of rosemary, or a little jar of the herb in a store or kitchen, to sniff it gently and for a brief fleeting moment to share an experience with Shakespeare.

HAREBELL

*. . . thou shalt not lack*
*The flower that's like thy face, pale*
*primrose, nor*
*The azured harebell, like thy veins.*

—CYMBELINE

The bell-shaped harebell is one of the most colorful of wild flowers, and is described by Shakespeare with his accustomed poetic touch. Azure blue is the deep blue which can be seen in the sky. A carpet of harebells spread under the trees must have been a familiar sight for Shakespeare as he walked about the countryside in spring. Today this flower is called wild hyacinth and what we know as "harebell" is a paler and more fragile wild flower. The names of flowers and their spellings have gone through many changes in their long history, especially where poetry is concerned, and the flowers in Shakespeare's plays are no exception. Persons of great honesty and sincerity are sometimes described as being "true-blue," and the poet William Brown, a contemporary of Shakespeare's, has also written about the harebell:

> *The Harebell for her stainless azured hue,*
> *Claims to be worn of none but those who are true.*
>
> —PASTORALS

We can be quite sure that Shakespeare had the color of the wild hyacinth in mind when he wrote of the "azured" blue of the harebell.

*Here's flowers for you;*
*Hot lavender, mints, savory, marjoram.*
—THE WINTER'S TALE

It is not difficult to imagine Shakespeare walking in his own garden, along the paved paths and between the colorful flower beds, when he wrote these lines for Perdita. It is amusing to note, though, that he is describing a typical English garden in the wild country of Bohemia where the scene actually takes place. The flowers are, she says, those "of middle summer" and "given to men of middle age." All of them are fragrant and full of flavor.

The smell of lavender is associated with freshness and cleanliness, and it is still used to perfume linen and cupboards where linen is stored, but we do not often hear about the *taste* of lavender. "Hot lavender" refers to its flavor when chewed, which is not unlike that of peppermint. No garden at any time has been complete without this sweet-smelling flower.

The history of savory goes back a long way in English history. It may have been brought to England by the Roman invaders, who valued it as an ingredient in spicy sauces and as a cure for bee stings.

WILD MARJORAM

CURLY MINT

SPEARMINT

60

Marjoram, which is still a popular herb in soups and salads and casseroles, appears several times in Shakespeare's plays. In *All's Well That Ends Well* we read of a "virtuous gentlewoman" who was "the sweet marjoram of the salad." Marjoram was also used as a "strewing herb" to keep floors clean and sweet smelling—which was by no means easy to do in those days.

It is plain that Shakespeare loved his herb garden and knew all about the plants that grew there. Other poets, writers, and herbalists of his time shared this knowledge, and this same little bunch of herbs appears many times in Elizabethan books about herbs and gardens.

Although we use fewer herbs today than did the goodwife in Stratford-upon-Avon, we *can* cook and eat a casserole or a pot roast that will taste much the same as one prepared four hundred years ago must have tasted.

LAVENDER

WINTER SAVORY

THYME
OXLIP
WOODBINE
MUSK-ROSE
EGLANTINE

*I know a bank where the wild thyme blows,*
*Where oxlips and the nodding violet grows*
*Quite over-canopied with luscious*
    *woodbine,*
*With sweet musk-roses and with eglantine.*
      —A MIDSUMMER NIGHT'S DREAM

*A Midsummer Night's Dream* is probably the first play of Shakespeare's to be read, seen, or acted in by most people; and King Oberon's speech to his fairy messenger Puck, beginning "I know a bank," must be one of the most familiar of all quotations from the plays. It is said that Shakespeare wrote this fairy play for the celebrations connected with a real wedding.

Sir Francis Bacon, the statesman and philosopher of Shakespeare's time, described the plant thyme in his essay "On Gardens" as being one of those that "perfume the air most delightfully, not passed by as the rest, but being trodden upon and crushed"; and he recommends it for garden paths. The fairies loved it, too, for its fragrance and chose it as a sweet-scented carpet upon which their queen, Titania, could lie and dream. It is easy to imagine just such a spot on the outskirts of the woods near Stratford-upon-Avon.

Thyme has always been beloved of the bees and was a symbol of sweetness. Delicious honey is made from its nectar. Ladies of the sixteenth and seventeenth centuries used to embroider scarves for their lovers with the design of a sprig of thyme over which hovered a bee. Thyme on the sea coast of England has been said by a modern poet to "smell like dawn in Paradise," and we cannot wonder that the fairies and the bees loved it.

There is a spell, at least as old as Shakespeare's time and possibly much older, in the Bodleian Library at Oxford, which enables one to see the "fayries." Among other plants needed to make the magic brew is wild thyme, "the tops of which must be gathered neare the side of a hill where fayries use to be oft, and the grass of a fayrie throne." Could this have been in Shakespeare's mind when he wrote "I know a bank where the wild thyme blows"?

The oxlip is a bright yellow flower, related to the cowslip and the primrose but taller and sturdier than either. In *The Winter's Tale* Perdita calls it "bold," and it makes a brave show in cottage gardens. It was very popular in Shakespeare's boyhood.

Honeysuckle, also called woodbine, was thought to be an emblem of affection and faithfulness. It grows in

*OXLIP*

64

*WILD THYME*

woods and hedges, and its sweet fragrance can be de-
tected from a distance, especially when it is basking in
the hot summer sun. For honeysuckle is a true plant of
midsummer, as are all the flowers in *A Midsummer Night's
Dream*. As its other name, woodbine, implies, it has a sec-
ond quality. It is a great climber and creeper, twisting its
many tendrils around the trunks of trees. This is described

by Shakespeare when the "doting" Queen Titania murmurs to poor bewitched Nick Bottom, the weaver,

*Sleep thou, and I will wind thee in my arms.*

.    .    .    .    .

*So doth the woodbine the sweet honeysuckle*
*Gently entwist,*

and seems to suggest that the tendrils of the creeping woodbine are twisted about its own blossom—the honeysuckle.

Honeysuckle was popular in Elizabethan gardens as a shade for bowers, covered walks, and paths. It grew thickly, giving both shelter and hiding place for lovers and secret meetings. In *Much Ado About Nothing* Hero bids her cousin, Beatrice, "steal into the pleached bower, where honeysuckles, ripen'd by the sun, forbid the sun to enter." A "pleached bower" or hedge was one where shrubs, bushes, or fruit trees had been cut back by the gardener to make a thick covered walk.

The true identity of the musk-rose in *A Midsummer*

*Night's Dream* has been in doubt for a long time. But to-day most authorities on roses agree that this sweet-scented flower is the "trailing rose" (*Rosa arvensis*) which blossoms in midsummer at the same time as the honey-suckle. It is deliciously fragrant, especially in the night air, and grows in woody places and hedges. Shakespeare refers to it again in the play when Queen Titania says to Bottom:

> *Come, sit thee down upon this flow'ry bed,*
> *While I thy amiable cheeks do coy,*
> *And stick musk-roses in thy sleek smooth head.*

With the musk-rose Shakespeare has entwined the eglantine, which is better known, perhaps, as sweet-briar, so popular in English cottage gardens. Its delicate scented leaves are scattered over the swooning Imogen in *Cymbeline*.

Eglantine is a little like the "sweet single rose" of New England which so delighted the hearts of the Pilgrims when they first saw it.

EGLANTINE
(sweet-briar)

68

MUSK-ROSE
(trailing rose)

WOODBINE
(honeysuckle)

69

# MARIGOLD

*The marigold, that goes to bed wi' the sun,*
*And with him rises weeping.*

—THE WINTER'S TALE

Shakespeare shared with many early poets the charming idea that the marigold closes its eyes with the sun and opens them again at sunrise. The words "and with him rises weeping" suggest the drops of morning dew on the petals of these gay golden flowers—a truly poetic image.

A famous authority on herbs and gardens in Shakespeare's time, Gervase Markham, had a receipt for a salad containing violets, primroses, and gillyflowers, and it is known that a salad for the royal table of Queen Elizabeth contained thirty-five different ingredients. It is no wonder that the sixteenth-century housewife cultivated her herbs with so much labor and loving care, not only to flavor soups and pies but also as cures for many kinds of sickness and injury. The marigold, for example, provided excellent ointment for the skin and was an ingredient in a lotion for sprains. Its petals dropped into a bowl of broth were said to "strengthen and comfort the heart."

Marigolds are sometimes called Mary-buds after the

Virgin Mary. In medieval times they were much valued by monks and nuns for their healing virtues. Some of the earliest herb gardens were to be found in monasteries and convents, which were a valuable source of medicine and healing in early days. The name Mary-buds appears in one of Shakespeare's many songs, this one from *Cymbeline*:

> *Hark! hark! the lark at heaven's gate sings,*
> *And Phoebus 'gins arise,*
> *His steeds to water at those springs*
> *On chalic'd flowers that lies;*
> *And winking Mary-buds begin*
> *To ope their golden eyes.*

*MARIGOLD*

72

DAFFODIL

*When daffodils begin to peer,*
*With heigh! the doxy, over the dale,*
*Why, then comes in the sweet o' the year.*
　　　　　　—THE WINTER'S TALE

73

The first Sunday in April is known as "Daffodil Sunday" in England, and people come from far and wide to the woods, fields, and orchards that surround the little village of Dymock, about ten miles from the cathedral city of Gloucester. There they gather daffodils for the London hospitals. The beautiful golden flowers are spread out like a rich carpet on hillsides and under the elm trees over many miles of the southern English countryside.

Poets have always loved to write about daffodils and in Shakespeare's time they had several names for them, such as "daffydown-dilly" and "daffodilly." It is thought, however, that the name came originally from a very old English word, *affodyle*, which means "that which comes early."

The lines quoted above are from a song sung by the rogue and peddler Autolycus in *The Winter's Tale*. Shakespeare only mentions daffodils three times; but when he does we find some of his most beautiful poetry. In the same play Perdita is acting as hostess for her foster father, the shepherd, at a gay pastoral celebration called "the feast of sheep-shearing." She welcomes her guests with flowers. She is sad that she cannot present them with the flowers of spring, such as

> *. . . daffodils,*
> *That come before the swallow dares, and take*
> *The winds of March with beauty,*

and reminds her guests of the sad story of Proserpina, who was kidnapped by the god Pluto, while she was picking lilies in the fields, and carried off as his captive to the Underworld. In her terror and despair, Proserpina let drop the lilies which, so Greek legend tells, turned to daffodils as they touched the earth. Just why the lilies in the story turned to daffodils as they fell to earth we do not know for certain. It may be associated with the belief, found in early plant lore, that those spring flowers that hang their heads, such as daffodils, violets, and snowdrops, symbolize grief and tears.

When Perdita describes the daffodils as taking "the winds of March with beauty," she uses the word "take" in the Elizabethan sense, meaning to charm or bewitch. Four hundred years ago the winds of March were no less keen and sharp than they are today, and the picture of fields of wild daffodils swaying gently on their long stalks in the wind is a pleasant one. We can see this lovely sight for ourselves, just as Shakespeare must have done, in the woods near his home in Warwickshire, not so many miles from the scene of Daffodil Sunday.

LILY

*Fresh tears*
*Stood on her cheeks as doth the honey-dew*
*Upon a gather'd lily almost withered.*
—TITUS ANDRONICUS

*Of Nature's gifts thou may'st with*
 *lilies boast*
*And with the half-blown rose.*
—KING JOHN

*To gild refined gold, to paint the lily.*
—KING JOHN

*MADONNA LILY*

77

In spite of its beauty, its slender grace and elegance, and its ancient history, Shakespeare did not write much about the lily except as a symbol of purity and of the finest quality of "whiteness," especially when describing the hands and fingers of his heroines. The tall white lily has always disputed with the rose for the right to be called "Queen of Flowers." We find this mentioned in *Henry VIII*, where sad Queen Katharine says: "Like the lily, that once was mistress of the field and flourish'd, I'll hang my head and perish." But even if the rose has won the crown, the lily is honored above all flowers by its dedication to the Virgin Mary.

# BIBLIOGRAPHY

*Suggested Further Reading*

BROWNLOW, MARGARET. *Herbs and the Fragrant Garden* (Darton, Longman & Todd, London, 1957).

*CHUTE, MARCHETTE. *Shakespeare of London* (E. P. Dutton & Co., New York, 1950).

DAVIS, WILLIAM S. *Life in Elizabethan Days* (Harper & Brothers, New York, 1930).

DOWDEN, ANNE O., AND THOMSON, R. *Roses* (Odyssey Library, New York, 1965).

*DOWDEN, EDWARD. *Shakespeare: His Mind and Art* (Capricorn Books, New York, 1962).

*DRINKWATER, JOHN. *Shakespeare* (Collier Books, New York, 1962).

ECCLES, MARK. *Shakespeare in Warwickshire* (University of Wisconsin Press, Madison, 1963).

FELSKO, ELSA. *A Book of Wild Flowers* (illus.) (Thomas Yoseloff, Inc., New York, 1956).

*GRANVILLE-BARKER, H., AND HARRISON, G. B. (eds.). *A Companion to Shakespeare Studies* (Doubleday & Company, Inc. [Anchor Books], Garden City, 1960).

GRIGSON, GEOFFREY. *The Englishman's Flora* (Phoenix House, London, 1955).

*HARRISON, G. B. (ed.). *The Elizabethan Journals* (Doubleday & Company, Inc. [Anchor Books], Garden City, 1965).

MARTIN, W. KEBLE. *The Concise British Flora* (Michael Joseph, London, 1965).

*OVID. *The Metamorphoses* (Mentor Books, New York, 1958).

ROHDE, ELEANOUR S. *Shakespeare's Wild Flowers* (Medici Society, London, 1963).

*ROWSE, A. L. *William Shakespeare* (Pocket Books, Inc., New York, 1960).

*SPURGEON, CAROLINE. *Shakespeare's Imagery and What It Tells Us* (Cambridge University Press, New York, 1965).

*STAUFFER, DONALD. *Shakespeare's World of Images* (Midland Books, Bloomington, Indiana, 1966).

*WILSON, JOHN DOVER (ed.). *Life in Shakespeare's England* (Penguin Books, Baltimore, 1944 [Cambridge University Press, 1911]).

## Other Sources

*ALEXANDER, PETER (ed.). *Studies in Shakespeare* (Oxford University Press, New York, 1964).

BEISLEY, SIDNEY. *Shakespeare's Gardens* (Longmans, Green, London, 1864).

BRASSINGTON, W. S. *Shakespeare's Homeland* (J. M. Dent & Sons, London, 1903).

CRANE, WALTER. *Flowers from Shakespeare's Gardens* (illus.), (Cassell & Co., London, 1909).

*CRUTTWELL, PATRICK. *The Shakespearian Moment* (The Modern Library, New York, 1960).

*DYER, T. F. THISTLETON. *Folk-Lore of Shakespeare* (Dover Publications, Inc., New York, 1966).

ELLACOMBE, H. N. *Plant-Lore of Shakespeare* (Edward Arnold, London, 1896).

FELLOWES, E. H. *English Madrigal Verse* (Oxford University Press, New York, 1919).

FOX, LEVI. *The Borough Town of Stratford-upon-Avon* (Stratford-upon-Avon, 1953).

*———. *The Shakespearian Gardens* (Jarrold & Sons, Norwich, England).

GERARDE [or GERARD], JOHN. *The Herball or General Historie of Plantes* (London, 1636).

GRIEVE, MRS. MAUD. *A Modern Herbal* (Harcourt, Brace & Company, New York, 1931).

GRINDON, L. H. *Shakespere Flora* (Palmer & Howe, Manchester, 1883).

*HATTON, RICHARD G. *Handbook of Plant and Floral Ornament* (Dover Publications, Inc., New York [originally published 1909]).

PARKINSON, JOHN. *Paradisi in Sole* (ed. of 1629, reprinted by Methuen & Co., London, 1904).

RALEIGH, WALTER, AND OTHERS (eds.). *Shakespeare's England* (vol. II, Oxford University Press, New York, 1917, reissued 1966).

ROBERTS, H. *English Gardens* (Britain in Pictures series), (William Collins Sons & Co., London, 1944).

SAVAGE, F. G. *Flora and Folk-Lore of Shakespeare* (E. J. Burrow & Co., London, 1923).

TAYLOR, G. M. *British Garden Flowers* (Britain in Pictures series), (William Collins Sons & Co., London, 1946).

THOMAS, GRAHAM S. *Climbing Roses, Old and New* (St. Martins Press, New York, 1966).

———. *Old Shrub Roses* (Phoenix House, London, 1955, and Branford Press, Newton Center, Mass., 1956).

*VAN DOREN, MARK. *Shakespeare* (Doubleday & Company, Inc. [Anchor Books], Garden City, 1953).

* Indicates paperback book.

# INDEX OF PLANTS

[Italic numbers (for example, *48*) indicate illustrations; roman arabic numbers (for example, 49) indicate text.]

# INDEX OF SHAKE-
# SPEAREAN SOURCES

# INDEX OF PLAYS
# AND POEMS

## ABOUT THE ILLUSTRATOR

Anne Ophelia Dowden is recognized as one of America's foremost botanical illustrators. Her work has been exhibited in many museums and galleries and has also been published in major magazines throughout the country.

As a child in Colorado she began her lifelong hobby of collecting and drawing specimens of native plants and insects, a hobby to which she now devotes her full time. She pursued her interest in art at the Carnegie Institute of Technology in Pittsburgh, Pennsylvania, and after graduation continued her studies in New York, where she has lived ever since. She has taught at Pratt Institute, and for twenty years was head of the Art Department of Manhattanville College.

Mrs. Dowden has both written and illustrated several books for young readers: *Look at a Flower* and *The Secret Life of a Flower* (both botanical studies) and *Roses* (a book of history and legend). Of *Shakespeare's Flowers* she writes: "It has required intensive but fascinating research to learn just what these familiar plants looked like in Shakespeare's day—what varieties were growing in the gardens of his contemporaries, and what wildlings were to be found in the countryside of England."

## ABOUT THE AUTHOR

Jessica Kerr lectures to garden clubs on the flower imagery in Shakespeare's plays, and is particularly interested in every aspect of English life in the sixteenth and seventeenth centuries. She was born in Dublin, was educated at Roedean School in England, and studied at the Royal College of Music in London for five years on an open scholarship for violin, graduating with the degree of A.R.C.M. Mrs. Kerr now lives in Clearwater Beach, Florida.